GETTING TO KNOW
Shakespeare

Grades 6 & Up

AUTHORS

Elody Rathgen and Pauline Scanlan

Cover Design:	Brenda DiAntonis
Artwork:	Geraldine Sloane
Designer:	Graphic Solutions
Editor:	Pauline Scanlan
U.S.A. Production:	James Edward Grace
U.S.A. Editor:	Eric Migliaccio

Published in the U.S.A. with permission from:

User Friendly Resource Enterprises Ltd
P.O. Box 1820
Christchurch, New Zealand
St Elmo Courts
47 Hereford Street

Teacher Created Resources, Inc.
6421 Industry Way
Westminster, CA 92683
www.teachercreated.com

ISBN-0-7439-3286-2

©2003 Teacher Created Resources, Inc.

Reprinted, 2005

Made in U.S.A.

User Friendly Resources specializes in publishing educational resources for teachers and students across a wide range of curriculum areas, at both primary and secondary levels. If you wish to know more about our resources, or if you think your resource ideas have publishing potential, please contact us at one of the addresses given.

Table of Contents

ACT ONE

Supernatural Shakespeare

ACT TWO

Crimes and Criminals

ACT THREE

Women of Words

Introduction

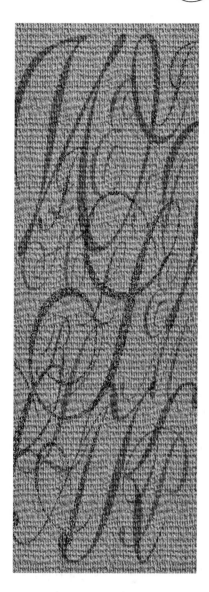

Recently, there has been renewed interest in introducing the works of Shakespeare to the general public. Film directors and actors from Britain, the United States, and Australia have been jumping on the Bard's bandwagon to re-package, re-interpret, re-shape, and re-invent a broad range of Shakespeare's works for a brand new audience: young people. If Shakespeare is working on the screen, it's up to us to make it work in the classroom.

At school, many of us can recall slogging through a seemingly impenetrable Shakespearean play taught by an uninspired teacher. If we were lucky, we might have come across a teacher who had a lively and enthusiastic approach to the Bard's work that captured our imaginations and laid the foundations for a love affair with Shakespeare's plays. If we were unlucky, we came out of school thinking Shakespeare was a waste of time, irrelevant, and/or too difficult.

Students shouldn't have to have a bad experience when they work with Shakespearean texts. The onus is on you, the teacher, to lay the foundations for that love affair. It's easy to teach Shakespeare badly: just hand out copies of a play and start reading. It's not so easy to teach it well. To teach Shakespeare well takes time for planning. Time is in short supply these days in schools—which is why *Getting to Know Shakespeare* can be a valuable resource.

This book examines a broad range of plays across three high-interest areas:

- The Supernatural
- Crimes and Criminals
- Women in Shakespeare

This book provides interesting and innovative approaches to working with snippets of text and will give you a good springboard from which to launch any in-depth work on specific plays that you might be contemplating. If you are working with younger students, see *Getting to Know Shakespeare* as providing them with a taste of joys to come. If you are working with older students, you will probably find material here that will link into whatever study you are planning; and it will also alert you to some new approaches to dealing with the texts.

The Prologue

To be, or not to be—that is the question.

—————— ᵉ - ᵉ ——————

Get thee to a nunnery.

—————— ᵉ - ᵉ ——————

Once more unto the breach, dear friends, once more.

—————— ᵉ - ᵉ ——————

A horse! a horse! my kingdom for a horse!

—————— ᵉ - ᵉ ——————

What's in a name? That which we call a rose
By any other name would smell as sweet.

—————— ᵉ - ᵉ ——————

When shall we three meet again? In thunder,
lightning, or in rain?

—————— ᵉ - ᵉ ——————

Out, damned spot, out I say!

—————— ᵉ - ᵉ ——————

All the perfumes of Arabia will not sweeten
this little hand.

—————— ᵉ - ᵉ ——————

Go, prick thy face, and over-red thy fear,
thou lily-livered boy!

—————— ᵉ - ᵉ ——————

All the world's a stage and all the men and
women merely players.

—————— ᵉ - ᵉ ——————

From forth the fatal loins of these two foes
A pair of star-cross'd lovers take their life.

FIND OUT

• *These quotations are some of Shakespeare's most famous lines. Do you know any others? See how many your class can come up with. Your teacher will help you out.*

• *How many of Shakespeare's play titles or characters do you know? Make another list.*

• *Prepare a wall display for your classroom during the time you are thinking about using this book, and fill it with things about Shakespeare. Put up the names of characters, plays, lines you like, memorable phrases, jokes, insults, unusual Shakespearean words, and other bits and pieces about the life and times of William Shakespeare. Make a brilliant display of your findings. Keep all this information up in your classroom. As you discover more about Shakespeare, add to your display. Check out film and play reviews, too.*

6

The Prologue (cont.)

Probably everyone in your class will have heard the name William Shakespeare. If you had to brainstorm something about him, you might be surprised how much information you already know about him and his work.

However, we must remember that William Shakespeare was born in England over 400 years ago, near the middle of the 16th century. He was an English playwright living in Tudor times. Yes, he has achieved great fame and recognition throughout history and across many cultures, but all cultures have their great artists: writers, storytellers, thinkers, painters, and so on. How many different cultures are represented in your classroom? Why not make it a class project to see how many other well-known writers, storytellers, poets, playwrights, and philosophers you can name from other cultures? You might have to ask at home for the names of these people. Collect as many names as you can. You could have a class list up on the wall. From which countries are these artists? How many women's names are there?

THINK

Why don't you try to brainstorm? Give everyone two minutes to think about anything that they associate with the name "Shakespeare," and then share, on a large piece of paper, all the collective knowledge the class has about Shakespeare. Are you impressed by the amount you already know?

The Prologue (cont.)

The following is a complete list of William Shakespeare's plays, divided into comedies, histories, and tragedies.

COMEDIES

All's Well That Ends Well

As You Like It

The Comedy of Errors

Cymbeline

Love's Labour's Lost

Measure for Measure

The Merry Wives of Windsor

The Merchant of Venice

A Midsummer Night's Dream

Much Ado About Nothing

Pericles, Prince of Tyre

The Taming of the Shrew

The Tempest

Troilus and Cressida

Twelfth Night, or What You Will

The Two Gentlemen of Verona

The Winter's Tale

HISTORIES

Henry IV, Part I

Henry IV, Part II

Henry V

Henry VI, Part I

Henry VI, Part II

Henry VI, Part III

Henry VIII

King John

Richard II

Richard III

TRAGEDIES

Antony and Cleopatra

Coriolanus

Hamlet

Julius Caesar

King Lear

Macbeth

Othello

Romeo and Juliet

Timon of Athens

Titus Andronicus

ACT ONE

 upernatural
hakespeare

The Unexplained and the Mysterious

ACT ONE

Supernatural Shakespeare

Do you have an interest in "the unexplained"—mysteries that no one seems to have found an answer to, like the Bermuda Triangle, poltergeists, or unidentified flying objects? You can probably think of lots more, and you might have your own strange stories to tell.

The curiosity that people have about these kinds of phenomena is not a new thing. For centuries, across all cultures, people have been fascinated by the possibility that there are elements of the world that cannot be explained by science or rational thought. This was certainly true in Shakespeare's day—although Shakespeare was living at a time when science and discovery were making great leaps forward (for example, the first ships left England for America, the "New World"). It was a time when many people still looked at the world through fearful and superstitious eyes.

The infant mortality rate was high, the "Black Death" was still abounding in Europe, and people's lives were short and often brutal. Most people were very religious, with a strong belief in heaven and hell. They felt that they had little control over their own destiny; they placed themselves in the hands of fate and fortune. They looked to fortune tellers, sought out "signs," followed astrology, and heeded stories about the supernatural to help them make sense of their lives. You might think that not much has changed!

THINK

Do you know people who read the "stars" in magazines or who visit palm readers? Are you interested in that kind of thing yourself? If you are, do you know why?

As an Elizabethan, the unexplained, the mysterious, and the supernatural were certainly part of Shakespeare's life. He was knowledgeable about and interested in the supernatural world and the ways in which that world had an effect on both ordinary people and people of rank, like kings and queens. It's possible that he had his own superstitions and beliefs about the workings of the supernatural world that we would find surprising today.

ACT ONE

Ghosts, Fairies, and Soothsayers

Supernatural Shakespeare

Elements of the unexplained, the mysterious, and the supernatural certainly found their way into many of Shakespeare's plays. To give you an idea, here is a selection of plays and some of the supernatural characters that appear in them:

Macbeth	three witches and a ghost
The Tempest	a magician and a spirit
Antony and Cleopatra	a fortune teller
A Midsummer Night's Dream	fairies and spirits
Hamlet	a ghost
Julius Caesar	a fortune teller
Richard III	ghosts
Henry VIII	spirits
Troilus and Cressida	a prophetess
Cymbeline	a fortune teller

GROUP WORK

In a small group, talk about what uses these sorts of characters might have in a play. You don't need to know anything about the plays, you just need to keep in mind that Shakespeare included them for a purpose. Why might some have names and others not?

You'll notice that these characters mostly fall into three categories: ghosts, fairies, and fortune tellers (or soothsayers). The ghosts and fairies (and also the witches in this case) belong in the realm of the supernatural; the fortune tellers (and the magician) can be classified as people with extraordinary powers. Some are named in the plays, like Cobweb, Moth, Peasebottom, and Mustardseed in *A Midsummer Night's Dream*; other characters are not.

What kinds of thoughts did you have in your discussion group? You might have decided that the main purpose of the ghosts was to scare the living daylights out of the audience or the other characters in the play—and you wouldn't be far wrong! However, many of these supernatural and mysterious characters also serve to provide other-worldly warnings to the play's main characters, like the soothsayer in *Julius Caesar*.

Sometimes they alert characters to wrongs that have been committed and that need to be put right, like the ghost in *Hamlet*. At other times, they play tricks on characters to make them look foolish and teach them a lesson or to give the audience a laugh, like the fairies and spirits in *A Midsummer Night's Dream*.

11

Mysterious Quotations

Below you will find some quotations that are related to the supernatural or mysterious from some of the plays we mentioned. In pairs, read them aloud and see if you can work out if what is said is:

—a warning to someone
_____

—said by someone who feels afraid
_____

—to make someone feel guilty
_____

—to stir someone into revenge
_____

—to make someone look silly
_____

ACT ONE

Supernatural Shakespeare

■ Fetch me that flower, the herb I show'd thee once:
The juice of it on sleeping eyelids laid
Will make or man or woman madly dote
Upon the next live creature that it sees.
... Having once this juice,
I'll watch Titania when she is asleep,
And drop the liquor of it in her eyes;
The next thing then she waking looks upon,
Be it on lion, bear, or wolf, or bull,
On meddling monkey, or on busy ape,
She shall pursue it with the soul of love.
(from _A Midsummer Night's Dream_)

■ Hence, horrible shadow!
Unreal mockery, hence!
(from _Macbeth_)

■ Let me sit heavy on thy soul tomorrow!
Think how thou stabb'dst me in my prime of youth
At Tewkesbury; despair, therefore and die!
(from _Richard III_)

■ If thou dost play with him at any game,
Thou are sure to lose;
(from _Antony and Cleopatra_)

■ The serpent that did sting thy father's life
Now wears his crown.
(from _Hamlet_)

ACT OUT

Speak the lines in a way that helps convey the meaning of the words. So, for example, if you decide one of the examples is meant as a warning, you might speak the words slowly and deliberately.

ACT ONE

Supernatural Shakespeare

Premonitions, Fate, and Strange Occurrences

Do you know what a premonition is? Have you ever had a sense that you knew something was going to happen? Perhaps you have had a dream that came true. Or you can sense when the telephone is about to ring. Shakespeare's characters often have premonitions, usually of a bad thing that's going to happen to them. If you have seen a performance of *Romeo and Juliet*—either on film, video, or on the stage—you will know that the story ends tragically: both Romeo and Juliet die unnecessarily. If you were listening to the story very carefully, as you watched you will have noticed that their impending deaths were signaled to the audience on several occasions throughout the play. For example, when Romeo is on his way to the Capulets' ball where he meets Juliet for the first time, he has a sudden premonition of what is to come; and although he quickly forgets about it, the audience doesn't.

THINK

If you were on your way to a party with a large group of your friends and you were worried that something bad could possibly happen there, would you still go to the party? Discuss this idea with a small group.

Benvolio	This wind you talk of blows us from ourselves. Supper is done, and we shall come too late.
Romeo	I fear too early, for my mind misgives Some consequence yet hanging in the stars Shall bitterly begin his fearful date With this night's revels, and expire the term Of a despised life clos'd in my breast By some vile forfeit of untimely death. *(Act 1, Scene 4)*

Premonitions, Fate, and Strange Occurrences (cont.)

ACT ONE

Supernatural **S**hakespeare

Later in the play, Romeo secretly marries Juliet but he gets into a fight with Tybalt, Juliet's cousin, on his way back from the church and kills him. For this crime, the Prince of Verona banishes Romeo to another city. Romeo and Juliet manage to spend a secret night together before he has to get out of town. As Romeo leaves Juliet's bedroom and climbs over the balcony to the garden below, she seems to have a vision of his death, and says:

Juliet
O God! I have an ill-divining soul,
Methinks I see thee, now thou art so low,
As one dead in the bottom of a tomb.
Either my eyesight fails, or thou look'st pale.

Romeo
And trust me, love, in my eye so do you—
(Act 3, Scene 5)

ACT OUT

Read these lines aloud with another person. Imagine that you are saying goodbye to someone you love very much (it might be a relative or a friend), when you have a sudden fear that you might never see them again. In pairs, write and then perform a "leave-taking" scene in which you show your concern for their leaving—but without making them feel as though they aren't able to go. Choose an appropriate setting and choose your words carefully. Be subtle, rather than overly dramatic. Don't try to copy Shakespeare's style. Use your own language.

#3286 *Getting to Know Shakespeare*

ACT ONE

*C*larence's Dream

In *Richard III*, the Duke of Clarence, brother of the Duke of Gloucester (who later becomes King Richard), is imprisoned in the Tower of London. Here is the story he tells to his guard (his Keeper) after a terrible nightmare. Read it aloud in pairs.

Keeper   Why looks your Grace so heavily to-day?

Clarence   O, I have pass'd a miserable night,
So full of fearful dreams, of ugly sights,
That, as I am a Christian faithful man,
I would not spend such another night
Though 'twere to buy a world of happy days,
So full of dismal terror was the time.

Keeper   What was your dream, my lord? I pray you, tell me.

Clarence   Methoughts that I had broken from the Tower,
And was embark'd to cross to Burgundy;
And in my company my brother Gloucester,
Who from my cabin tempted me to walk
Upon the hatches: there we look'd toward England,
And cited up a thousand heavy times,
During the wars of York and Lancaster,
That had befall'n us. As we pac'd along
Upon the giddy footing of the hatches,
Methought that Gloucester stumbled; and in falling,
Struck me, that thought to stay him, overboard,
Into the tumbling billows of the main.
O Lord, methought what pain it was to drown:
What dreadful noise of waters within mine ears!
What sights of ugly death within mine eyes!
Methoughts I saw a thousand fearful wracks;
A thousand men that fishes gnaw'd upon;
Wedges of gold, great anchors, heaps of pearl,
Inestimable stones, unvalu'd jewels,

*S*upernatural *S*hakespeare

Clarence's Dream (cont.)

All scatter'd in the bottom of the sea,
Some lay in dead men's skulls, and in those
holes
Where eyes did once inhabit, there were crept,
As 'twere in scorn of eyes, reflecting gems,
That woo'd the slimy bottom of the deep,
And mock'd the dead bones that lay
scatter'd by.

(Act I, Scene 4)

Supernatural Shakespeare

In Clarence's dream, he imagines ("methought") that his evil brother, the Duke of Gloucester, stumbles into him on the deck of a ship bound for France ("Burgundy") and knocks him into the sea, where he dies.

Soon after Clarence has told his dream to the guard, he is set upon by two murderers who have been sent by his brother, Gloucester. They stab him and drown him in a vat of wine. In some productions, he is shown as being drowned in his own bath. From this, you can probably see that the general feel of Clarence's premonition is correct, although the real circumstances are not the same as the dream. His actual death is much less "poetic" and more brutal. In his dream, he even has time to look at sights beneath the ocean as he drowns! In reality, although he dies bravely, trying to argue his case rationally with the men who come to kill him, his is a very ugly and "ignoble" end.

DESIGN WORK

Look back through Clarence's dream and highlight the parts of the dream that might be well represented by visual images.

Then consider how Clarence actually dies (if you want to read this part of the play for yourselves look at Act 1, Scene 4). Design a large image that shows the differences and similarities between the dream and the reality of Clarence's death. You might make the image multi-media and even include words from the scene to draw out the differences and similarities.

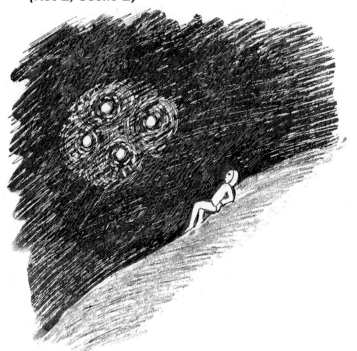

ACT ONE

Written in the Stars

Supernatural Shakespeare

Although Shakespeare makes us aware through his characters that he was familiar with the beliefs of the times, he does not indicate his own point of view on these matters. It is not uncommon for characters in his plays to present contradictory arguments. For example, at the very start of *Romeo and Juliet*, the prologue sets out the whole course of the story for us:

> From forth the fatal loins of these two foes
> A pair of star-cross'd lovers take their life,

Here the words "star-crossed lovers" show that the fate of the two lovers is somehow tied up with the stars, or astrology. In other words, the fate of the pair has already been sealed by a force beyond their control. However, Edmund, in *King Lear*, mocks astrology and the unreliability of its predictions:

Edmund   This is the excellent foppery of the world, that when we are sick in fortune—often the surfeits of our own behavior—we make guilty of our disasters the sun, the moon, and the stars.

(Act 1, Scene 2)

THINK

As a class, consider the idea that our destinies are "already written." By this we mean that our futures have already been planned; that all we need to do is to play a part in the drama of our lives as they unfold—and from time to time we might get a look, like Clarence in his dream, at what's in store for us. Where do individuals in the class stand on this idea? Are our destinies already "hanging in the stars" from the day we are born, or do we play a part in the shaping of our own futures?

The "Weird Sisters"

One play in which Shakespeare brings together a whole raft of supernatural forces and strange occurrences is *Macbeth*. Set in the dark and forbidding Scottish highlands, it tells the story of a great Scottish warrior, Macbeth, who is stopped by three witches as he makes his way home from a battle. They prophesy that he will become King of Scotland. Macbeth goes on to ensure that the prophecy comes true by murdering his way to the top job. The audience is left to ponder whether Macbeth would have become king if he had never met the witches and been driven to murder by his own ambition and impatience.

The witches in the story are intended to be very fearsome. Unlike the sprites and fairies found in most of his other plays (who are often meddlesome and mischievous, but not malevolent), these characters are full of treachery and evil. During the years in which Shakespeare was writing, belief in witches was common, especially in rural places. If children were born with deformities or crops failed, people sometimes looked to unusual or "different" people in their communities for the cause. For example, women who lived alone were a prime target. These people were reviled and often put to death—although most were completely harmless.

With the three witches who open up the first scene in *Macbeth*, Shakespeare tapped into the deep-seated fears of many uneducated Elizabethan playgoers. There is nothing comfortable or homely about these three women. In the opening scene, their rhymes and incantations are accompanied by thunder and lightning. They meet on deserted moorland (open wasteland overgrown with shrubs) and in caves. Their craft is dark, and their words are tinged with hints of their associations with otherworldly beings, "our masters." Their supernatural powers anchor the progress of the story.

PRODUCTION ACTIVITY

Look at this scene from Act 4 in the play. Macbeth has already killed the king and been pronounced king himself. But he is afraid that his success and security might be short-lived. He visits the witches to ask what is in store for him in the future. So far, to try and secure his position as king, he has also murdered one of his most loyal soldiers, Banquo.

When he finds the witches in a cave, they are expecting him and have been preparing a cauldron of unspeakable ingredients to use in a spell. On stage or on film, this can be one of the most terrifying scenes in the play.

ACT ONE

supernatural Shakespeare

ACT ONE

Supernatural Shakespeare

READ THROUGH

With your teacher, read through the scene. Before you talk about it, write down what you think is happening. Also, make a note of any lines you had difficulty following. After this, as a class discuss the points you made and questions you had.

• *In groups, give out the following parts:*

Macbeth

First Witch

Second Witch

Third Witch

First Apparition (a head encased in armour)

Second Apparition (a child covered in blood)

Third Apparition (a child wearing a crown and holding a branch or small tree)

Lennox (a lord who comes to find Macbeth)

• *Read through the scene again and, as you read, think about how you can create an atmosphere of fear and terror (for the audience) in your use of language. Try to make each part seem different, and don't fall into the trap of "hamming it up." Next, walk through the part and make some decisions about how you would stage it. Make a note of these decisions. You need to think about the audience at all times. Ensure that they can hear and understand what you say, and plan how you will be positioned so that they can see and hear what is happening.*

Second Witch   By the pricking of my thumbs,
Something wicked this way comes.
Open, locks,
Whoever knocks

[Enter Macbeth]

Macbeth   How now, you secret, black, and midnight hags?
What is't you do?

All   A deed without a name.

Macbeth I conjure you, by that which you profess,
            Howe'er you come to know it—answer me,
            Though you untie the winds and let them fight
            Against the churches; though the yesty waves
            Confound and swallow navigation up;
            Though bladed corn be lodg'd and trees blown down;
            Though castles topple on their warders' heads;
            Though palaces and pyramids do slope
            Their heads to their foundations; though the treasure
            Of nature's germens tumble all together,
            Even till destruction sicken; answer me
            To what I ask you.

First Witch Speak.

Second Witch Demand.

Third Witch We'll answer.

First Witch Say, if thou'dst rather hear it from our mouths,
            Or from our masters?

Macbeth Call 'em; let me see 'em.

First Witch Pour in sow's blood, that hath eaten
            Her nine farrow; grease, that's sweaten
            From the murderer's gibbet, throw
            Into the flame.

            All   Come, high or low;
            Thy self and office deftly show.

[Thunder. First Apparition: an armed Head]

ACT ONE

Supernatural Shakespeare

Macbeth   Tell me, thou unknown power—

First Witch   He knows thy thought:
Hear his speech, but say thou nought.

First Apparition   Macbeth! Macbeth!
Macbeth! Beware Macduff;
Beware the Thane of Fife. Dismiss me. Enough.

[He descends.]

Macbeth   Whate'er thou art, for thy good caution, thanks;
Thou hast harp'd my fear aright. But one word more—

First Witch   He will not be commanded. Here's another,
More potent than the first.

[Thunder. Second Apparition: Bloody Child]

Second Apparition   Macbeth! Macbeth! Macbeth!

Macbeth   Had I three ears, I'd hear thee.

21

Second
Apparition Be bloody, bold, and resolute; laugh to scorn.

The power of man; for none of woman born

Shall harm Macbeth.

[Descends]

Macbeth Then live, Macduff; what need I fear of thee?

But yet I'll make assurance double sure,

And take a bond of fate. Thou shalt not live;

That I may tell pale-hearted fear it lies,

And sleep in spite of thunder.

[Thunder. Third Apparition: a Child Crowned, with a tree in his hand]

What is this,

That rises like the issue of a king,

And wears upon his baby brow the round

And top of sovereignty?

All Listen, but speak not to't.

Third
Apparition Be lion-mettled, proud, and take no care

Who chafes, who frets, or where conspirers are.

Macbeth shall never vanquish'd be until

Great Birnam wood to high Dunsinane hill

Shall come against him.

[Descends]

Macbeth That will never be:

Who can impress the forest, bid the tree

Unfix his earth-bound root? Sweet bodements! Good!

Rebellious head, rise never till the wood

Of Birnam rise, and our high-placed Macbeth

Shall live the lease of nature, pay his breath

To time and mortal custom. Yet my heart

ACT ONE

upernatural hakespeare

ACT ONE

Supernatural Shakespeare

PRODUCTION

If you were preparing this scene to produce at a school's drama festival, how would you deal with staging, costuming, and the need for special effects? You might like to annotate (write notes alongside) this scene, design a stage set on paper with annotations, or build a small model of the set and write accompanying notes.

	Throbs to know one thing: tell me, if your art
	Can tell so much: shall Banquo's issue ever
	Reign in this kingdom?
All	Seek to know no more.
Macbeth	I will be satisfied. Deny me this,
	And an eternal curse fall on you! Let me know.
	Why sinks that cauldron? And what noise is this?

[Hautboys]

First Witch	Show!
Second Witch	Show!
Third Witch	Show!
All	Show his eyes, and grieve his heart;
	Come like shadows, so depart.

[A show of eight Kings, the last with a glass in his hand; GHOST OF BANQUO following]

Macbeth	Thou art too like the spirit of Banquo; down!
	Thy crown does sear mine eyeballs. And thy hair,
	Thou other gold-bound brow, is like the first.
	A third is like the former. Filthy hags!
	Why do you show me this?—A fourth? Start, eyes!
	What, will the line stretch out to the crack of doom?
	Another yet! A seventh? I'll see no more.
	And yet the eighth appears, who bears a glass
	Which shows me many more; and some I see
	That twofold balls and treble scepters carry.
	Horrible sight! Now, I see, 'tis true,

For the blood-bolter'd Banquo smiles upon me,
And points at them for his.

[Apparitions vanish]

What, is this so?

First Witch Ay, sir, all this is so. But why
Stands Macbeth thus amazedly?
Come, sisters, cheer we up his sprites,
And show the best of our delights.
I'll charm the air to give a sound,
While you perform your antic round.
That this great king may kindly say,
Our duties did his welcome pay.

[Music. The witches dance and then vanish]

Macbeth Where are they? Gone? Let this pernicious hour
Stand aye accursed in the calendar!
Come in, without there!

[Enter Lennox]

Lennox What's your grace's will?

Macbeth Saw you the weird sisters?

Lennox No, my lord.

Macbeth Came they not by you?

Lennox No indeed, my lord.

Macbeth Infected be the air whereon they ride,
And damn'd all those that trust them!

(Act 4, Scene 1)

ACT ONE

Supernatural Shakespeare

Writing the Scenery

One of the things that Shakespeare had to do in his plays was actually describe the scenery, the weather, and the time of day, because in his time theaters could not provide all the special effects to show the audience what was happening. There was no lighting, of course, no sound system, and very little scenery was able to be put on stage. Sometimes a throne would be used to show that the scene was in a palace.

In *Hamlet,* for example, Shakespeare used some interesting descriptions to give us an idea of the time of day. Look at the end of Act 1, Scene 1, where some guards who have been on duty all night know that the end of their watch has come when one says:

> But look, the morn in russet mantle clad,
> Walks o'er the dew of yon high eastward hill.

Try to put this description of dawn breaking in your own language.

_____

_____

Here is another quotation from *Hamlet*:

> 'Tis now the very witching time of night,
> When churchyards yawn and hell itself breathes out
> Contagion to this world. Now could I drink hot blood,
> And do such bitter business as the day
> Would quake to look on.
> **(Act 3, Scene 2)**

How vivid this description is! What time does it describe?

What do the different images mean to you?

Writing the Scenery (cont.)

ACT ONE

Supernatural
Shakespeare

WRITE AND DESIGN

*Now, choose a time of day that you enjoy and try
to write two or three sentences describing it
without actually saying the hour. Use lively,
imaginative, and expressive language as
Shakespeare has. Read your sentences out to each
other and see if people can tell what time you
mean. How accurate are they? Later, you might
put these descriptions on larger sheets of paper,
perhaps with some design work to set them off,
and then display them around the wall.
Shakespeare's examples could go on display too.
What time of day did your teacher describe?*

#3286 Getting to Know Shakespeare

©Teacher Created Resources, Inc.

ACT TWO

Crimes and Criminals

Murder, Mayhem, and Revenge

Among some of the most popular entertainments today are crime and police stories. Whether as books, television series, or films, detective mysteries, suspense, and crime-solving stories attract huge audiences.

What do people enjoy about such programs or stories? Is it the excitement of trying to guess who did it (or "who dunnit")? Or is it a sense of interest in people getting justice? What other reasons could there be? Share as many as you can around your group. You might do a survey as a class to find out why people enjoy these kinds of stories so much.

In the best of these programs, the ones people in your class have said they enjoy, what are the things that make them so enjoyable? Draw up a table to show what the most common factors are making for successful crime dramas.

Crimes and Criminals

Since the times of Seneca, a Latin playwright from 4 B.C.–65 A.D., such writing has always been popular. What people enjoyed about crime stories in those days were the details of the crime itself, the nature of the criminal characters, the theme of revenge, and the ways in which people, without realizing it at first, became involved in the crime or were tricked into being accomplices. Sometimes the crime was an act of revenge for a previous crime. Many of these early works focused on the bloodiness and violence of the crime acts. This is what people seemed to enjoy.

Is this different from or similar to your survey results of what people today look for in a successful mystery or crime story?

THINK

Name some of the most popular crime or police programs, writers, or characters. If you have some personal favorites, note them as well.

Are there particular character types that emerge in these stories? Can you identify them?

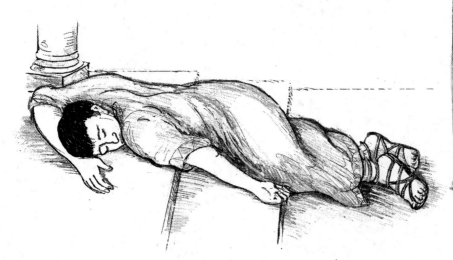

ACT TWO

Crimes and Criminals

The Revenge Story

William Shakespeare had a very good sense of what audiences enjoyed; and during his time, the revenge story was popular. He often borrowed plot details from well-known revenge and mystery stories that he knew would attract people, but then he added other material and developed his own ideas and characters to make new plays out of old favorites. The famous *Hamlet* is one of the best examples of a revenge story. Here is a brief outline:

> Hamlet's father, the king of Denmark, dies suddenly and somewhat mysteriously. Very soon after the funeral, Hamlet's mother remarries. Her new husband is the former king's brother, Claudius. Hamlet is upset by the quick remarriage, and in his distressed state sees what appears to be his father's ghost. He becomes convinced that Claudius is, in fact, the murderer of his father.
>
> He devises a plan to appear to be mad (insane) so that he can investigate the situation under cover. In this state, he rejects his girlfriend, Ophelia, who goes crazy and dies. He alienates her brother Laertes, at one time his friend, who then plots with Claudius, who is by now king, to get rid of Hamlet. Although he feels sure that Claudius is the murderer of the former king, Hamlet delays taking action. This gives Claudius time to put his murderous schemes in place, and, in a dramatic climax, all the major characters die: Laertes and Hamlet are poisoned by a lethal concoction put on the tip of Laertes's sword for the duel; Hamlet's mother drinks a poisonous chalice of wine (meant for Hamlet not her); and in his dying moment, Hamlet manages to fatally stab Claudius.

PRODUCTION ACTIVITY

In groups, take one aspect of the *Hamlet* story and plan a short scene around it—just a short take of 2 or 3 minutes. You might give it a modern setting, or you might set it back in an earlier time. Since you have been given only the bare bones of *Hamlet's* story, you will have to add details which you make up yourself. You will need to think more about the characters, as well to develop what they are like. Plan your scene, keeping in mind the ideas you have discussed about successful crime stories. Your scene might focus on what happens to Ophelia, or it might be a scene between Hamlet and his mother, or perhaps something about Claudius's plotting to kill Hamlet. You will also have ideas of your own for other scenes.

The Revenge Story (cont.)

ACT TWO

Several films have been made of Shakespeare's play *Hamlet*, including one starring Mel Gibson, another with Kenneth Branagh, and a famous one with the actor Sir Laurence Olivier taking on the title role. Ask your teacher to show you from one of the films some scenes that are similar to the scenes you have developed, practiced, and performed in your class.

After you have enjoyed viewing the scenes, you could discuss what similarities and differences there are between your scenes and the ones in the film. One topic for the discussion might be the language Shakespeare uses. In addition to looking at some of the film scenes, ask your teacher to show you some copies of extracts from the scenes, so that you can read Shakespeare's language for yourselves. What are some differences that you notice compared with the language that you used in your scenes?

Crimes and Criminals

WRITING GROUPS

A typical revenge story of the period contained these elements, all of which can be found in *Hamlet*:

- a villain
- a complex plot
- a ghost
- a suffering heroine
- lust
- torture and/or poisoning
- madness
- a play within a play
- characters of high rank
- murders

Choose a number of these elements and work out an outline for your own revenge story.

©*Teacher Created Resources, Inc.*

ACT TWO

Moral Dilemmas

Crimes and Criminals

Today we have very well-defined justice systems that set out clearly not only what actions are criminal but also what rights people have. We are very careful about what powers the police force can use and about the rules by which lawyers should conduct their cases. Consideration has been given to what penalties should be handed down when someone is found guilty. There is a lot of emphasis on making sure the law is fair to everyone, no matter their age or culture, whether they are rich or poor, man or woman. There are technological and scientific processes that can be used to track criminals, even when the evidence is difficult to find and the criminal very skillful.

But policing and the law have not always been as carefully monitored as they now are. In the past it was more difficult to find and track criminals because there weren't such sophisticated technologies and international communications to catch them. On the other hand, in the past, since people lived in much smaller towns and communities, they knew each other better, so it was harder to be anonymous or to go unnoticed. Strangers or odd events were quickly noticed and discovered.

Our ideas about crime and justice, guilt, revenge, and responsibility have always been the subject of much discussion and debate. Many cases remain unsolved, and many people found guilty of crimes continue to protest that they are innocent until the day of their deaths. There are many such famous cases in this country and overseas. You might take the opportunity with your teacher to read and investigate some of these famous stories. Keep an eye on your local newspaper for the current court proceedings.

Sometimes the idea of guilt and innocence is not easily determined. It might be easy to pronounce that someone committed an illegal act—but what of the circumstances surrounding that act? What if someone stole to feed their family? What if someone killed to protect themselves?

$\mathcal{M}$oral Dilemmas *(cont.)*

Here are some discussion ideas that you might use in groups or as a class to begin considering as moral dilemmas. Moral dilemmas are problems which can be viewed from many different positions and that do not have easy answers. Maybe on some of these matters you will not be able to agree at all. As well as discussing them in groups, you might use them for debate topics or for pieces of thoughtful essay writing.

- What sorts of actions do we consider criminal? Are there occasions when those actions might not be considered criminal?

- What sorts of situations make one crime worse than another?

- Is it useful to rank crimes in order of seriousness? Can you agree on a list? If not, what are the reasons causing your disagreements?

- Would we call something a crime if everyone involved were partly guilty?

- If a person is "made to do a crime" because someone else gives them wrong information, should they be held responsible for it?

- When should we try to stop a friend from committing a crime?

- Can the justice system itself sometimes be guilty of unfairness?

ACT TWO

$\mathcal{C}$rimes and $\mathcal{C}$riminals

CLARIFYING SOME LANGUAGE

Before you read the following scene, discuss your understandings of these terms and expressions. Write some sentences to show how they can be used in the context of the law:

- the letter of the law _____

- the spirit of justice _____

- mercy _____

- judgement _____

- sentence _____

- pardon _____

In most societies, the law is seen to be above influence. It is supposed to offer everyone a fair opportunity in a public setting to have justice done, to have "their day in court." Shakespeare's plays *The Merchant of Venice* and *Measure for Measure* both have themes that focus on the administration of justice and the consequences of how the sentence of the courts affect people's lives.

ACT TWO

Crimes and Criminals

From The Merchant of Venice

The story so far:

Bassanio has had to borrow money from his friend Antonio, a wealthy Venetian merchant. Because Antonio's money is all tied up in a big commercial venture, he has no available cash and so he borrows money from a moneylender, Shylock, to help his friend out. In those days, lending money was not a reputable business and was often handled by members of the Jewish community. Shylock is well-known as a difficult man who has made a lot of money from his unpopular business. He and Antonio have never been the best of friends. In their written agreement about the money to be lent, they state that, if Antonio cannot repay the bond in time, Shylock will take pound of flesh from Antonio by way of repayment.

Antonio is so sure of his business success that he sees the unusual agreement as a bit of a joke. However, in a disastrous turn of events, Antonio's venture is delayed and he has no money to repay on the agreed date. Attempts are made, through the justice system, to get the agreement overturned, but in the courtroom Shylock is unmovable about his right to his bond. Portia, who is engaged to Bassanio, is the lawyer attempting to change Shylock's mind. (She is, of course, in disguise as a young man, since women could not hold any public office in those days!) Her first appeal, in one of Shakespeare's most famous speeches, is to Shylock's sense of mercy. But he cannot be moved. She then turns to the "letter of the law."

CLARIFYING THE STORY

Some other things you need to know to help you follow and respond to the situation are that:

- Antonio and Shylock have a history of conflict, with Antonio being publicly critical of Shylock in the past for being a moneylender and charging interest.

- Shylock is a very proud Jewish man who has suffered abuse and racism from many people. He is broken-hearted that his daughter, Jessica, has run off with a Christian man, Lorenzo, to get married.

- Earlier in the play, Shylock has expressed his deep feelings about the way in which he is often caused to suffer at the hands of the Christians, and that he has learned by their example to be hard-hearted. Here is the speech in which he explains how he has been harassed and mistreated by others:

Crimes and Criminals

Shylock   *(with reference to Antonio)*

He hath disgraced me, and hindered me half a million, laughed at my losses, mocked at my gains, scorned my nation, thwarted my bargains, cooled my friends, heated mine enemies; and what's his reason? I am a Jew. Hath not a Jew eyes? Hath not a Jew hands, organs, dimensions, senses, affections, passions, fed with the same food, hurt with the same weapons, subject to the same diseases, healed by the same means, warmed and cooled by the same winter and summer, as a Christian is? If you prick us, do we not bleed? If you tickle us, do we not laugh? If you poison us, do we not die? And if you wrong us, shall we not revenge? If we are like you in the rest, we will resemble you in that. If a Jew wrong a Christian, what is his humility? Revenge. If a Christian wrong a Jew, what should his sufferance be by Christian example? Why, revenge. The villainy you teach me I will execute, and it shall go hard but I will better the instruction.

(Act 3, Scene 1)

ACT TWO

Crimes and Criminals

THE COURT SCENE

Duke   You hear the learn'd Bellario, what he writes:
And here, I take it, is the doctor come.

[Enter PORTIA, dressed like a doctor of laws]

Give me your hand. Come you from old Bellario?

Portia   I did, my lord.

Duke   You are welcome: take your place.
Are you acquainted with the difference
That holds this present question in the court?

Portia   I am informed thoroughly of the cause.
Which is the merchant here, and which the Jew?

Duke   Antonio and old Shylock, both stand forth.

Portia   Is your name Shylock?

Shylock   Shylock is my name.

Portia   Of a strange nature is the suit you follow;
Yet in such rule that the Venetian law
Cannot impugn you as you do proceed.
You stand within his danger, do you not?

READ THROUGH

Read through this court scene (in groups first) to work out what is happening. (The Duke is the judge in the courtroom; Portia is in disguise and nobody knows her real identity; Gratiano is a friend and supporter of Bassanio and Antonio.)

ACT TWO

Antonio   Ay, so he says.

Portia   Do you confess the bond?

Antonio   I do.

Portia   Then must the Jew be merciful.

Shylock   On what compulsion must I?
Tell me that.

Portia   The quality of mercy is not strain'd,
It droppeth as the gentle rain from heaven
Upon the place beneath: it is twice bless'd
It blesseth him that gives and him that takes:
'Tis mightiest in the mightiest; it becomes
The throned monarch better than his crown;
His sceptre shows the force of temporal
power,
The attribute to awe and majesty,
Wherein doth sit the dread and fear of kings;
But mercy is above this sceptred sway,
It is enthroned in the hearts of kings,
It is an attribute to God himself,
And earthly power doth then show
likest God's
When mercy seasons justice.
Therefore, Jew,
Though justice be thy plea, consider
this,
That, in the course of justice, none
of us
Should see salvation: we do pray for
mercy,

Crimes and Criminals

ACT TWO

Crimes and Criminals

And that same prayer doth teach us all to render
The deeds of mercy. I have spoke thus much
To mitigate the justice of thy plea,
Which if thou follow, this strict court of Venice
Must needs give sentence 'gainst the merchant there.

Shylock   My deeds upon my head! I crave the law,
The penalty and forfeit of my bond.

Portia   Is he not able to discharge the money?

Bassanio   Yes, here I tender it for him in the court;
Yea, twice the sum: if that will not suffice,
I will be bound to pay it ten times o'er,
On forfeit of my hands, my head, my heart.
If this will not suffice, it must appear
That malice bears down truth. And I beseech you,
Wrest once the law to your authority:
To do a great right, do a little wrong,
And curb this cruel devil of his will.

Portia   It must not be. There is no power in Venice
Can alter a decree established:
'Twill be recorded for a precedent,
And many an error by the same example
Will rush into the state. It cannot be.

Shylock   A Daniel come to judgment! Yea, a Daniel!
O wise young judge, how I do honour thee!

ACT TWO

Crimes and Criminals

Portia   I pray you, let me look upon the bond.

Shylock   Here 'tis, most reverend doctor; here it is.

Portia   Shylock, there's thrice thy money offer'd thee.

Shylock   An oath, an oath, I have an oath in heaven:
Shall I lay perjury upon my soul?
No, not for Venice.

Portia   Why, this bond is forfeit;
And lawfully by this the Jew may claim
A pound of flesh, to be by him cut off
Nearest the merchant's heart. Be merciful:
Take thrice thy money; bid me tear the bond.

Shylock   When it is paid according to the tenor.
It doth appear you are a worthy judge;
You know the law, your exposition
Hath been most sound: I charge you by the law,
Whereof you are a well-deserving pillar,
Proceed to judgment: by my soul I swear
There is no power in the tongue of man
To alter me: I stay here on my bond.

Antonio   Most heartily I do beseech the court
To give the judgment.

Portia   Why then, thus it is:
You must prepare your bosom for his knife.

ACT TWO

Crimes and Criminals

Shylock	O noble judge! O excellent young man!
Portia	For the intent and purpose of the law Hath full relation to the penalty, Which here appeareth due upon the bond.
Shylock	'Tis very true! O wise and upright judge! How much more elder art thou than thy looks!
Portia	Therefore lay bare your bosom.
Shylock	Ay, "his breast": So says the bond—doth it not, noble judge?— "Nearest his heart": those are the very words.
Portia	It is so. Are there balance here to weigh The flesh?
Shylock	I have them ready.
Portia	Have by some surgeon, Shylock, on your charge, To stop his wounds, lest he do bleed to death.
Shylock	Is it so nominated in the bond?

Portia	It is not so express'd; but what of that? 'Twere good you do so much for charity.
Shylock	I cannot find it: 'tis not in the bond.
Portia	You, merchant, have you any thing to say?
Antonio	But little: I am arm'd and well prepared. Give me your hand, Bassanio: fare you well! Grieve not that I am fallen to this for you; For herein Fortune shows herself more kind Than is her custom: it is still her use To let the wretched man outlive his wealth, To view with hollow eye and wrinkled brow An age of poverty; from which lingering penance Of such misery doth she cut me off. Commend me to your honourable wife: Tell her the process of Antonio's end; Say how I lov'd you, speak me fair in death; And, when the tale is told, bid her be judge Whether Bassanio had not once a love. Repent but you that you shall lose your friend, And he repents not that he pays your debt; For if the Jew do cut but deep enough, I'll pay it presently with all my heart.

ACT TWO

Crimes and Criminals

ACT TWO

Crimes and Criminals

Bassanio Antonio, I am married to a wife
Which is as dear to me as life itself;
But life itself, my wife, and all the world,
Are not with me esteem'd above thy life:
I would lose all, ay, sacrifice them all
Here to this devil, to deliver you.

Portia Your wife would give you little thanks for that,
If she were by to hear you make the offer.

Gratiano I have a wife, whom, I protest, I love:
I would she were in heaven, so she could
Entreat some power to change this currish
Jew.

Nerissa 'Tis well you offer it behind her back;
The wish would make else an unquiet house.

Shylock These be the Christian husbands! I have
a daughter;
Would any of the stock of Barrabas
Had been her husband rather than a Christian!

[Aside]

We trifle time: I pray thee, pursue sentence.

Portia A pound of that same merchant's flesh is
thine:
The court awards it, and the law doth give it.

Shylock Most rightful judge!

Portia And you must cut this flesh from off his
breast:
The law allows it, and the court awards it.

Shylock Most learned judge! A sentence!
Come, prepare!

©*Teacher Created Resources, Inc.*   *#3286 Getting to Know Shakespeare*

Portia   Tarry a little; there is something else.
This bond doth give thee here no jot of blood;
The words expressly are "a pound of flesh"
Take then thy bond, take thou thy pound of flesh;
But, in the cutting it, if thou dost shed
One drop of Christian blood, thy lands and goods
Are, by the laws of Venice, confiscate
Unto the state of Venice.

Gratiano   O upright judge! Mark, Jew: O learned judge!

Shylock   Is that the law?

Portia   Thyself shalt see the act;
For, as thou urgest justice, be assur'd
Thou shalt have justice, more than thou desir'st.

Gratiano   O learned judge! Mark, Jew: a learned judge!

Shylock   I take this offer then: pay the bond thrice,
And let the Christian go.

Bassanio   Here is the money.

Portia   Soft!
The Jew shall have all justice; soft! no haste:
He shall have nothing but the penalty.

Gratiano   O Jew! an upright judge, a learned judge!

ACT TWO

Crimes and Criminals

ACT TWO

Crimes and Criminals

Portia   Therefore prepare thee to cut off the flesh.
Shed thou no blood, nor cut thou less nor more,
But just a pound of flesh: if thou tak'st more,
Or less, than a just pound, be it but so much
As makes it light or heavy in the substance,
Or the division of the twentieth part
Of one poor scruple, nay, if the scale do turn
But in the estimation of a hair,
Thou diest and all thy goods are confiscate.

Gratiano   A second Daniel, a Daniel, Jew!
Now, infidel, I have you on the hip.

Portia   Why doth the Jew pause? Take thy forfeiture.

Shylock   Give me my principal, and let me go.

Bassanio   I have it ready for thee; here it is.

Portia   He hath refus'd it in the open court:
He shall have merely justice, and his bond.

Gratiano   A Daniel, still say I; a second Daniel!
I thank thee, Jew, for teaching me that word.

Shylock   Shall I not have barely my principal?

Portia   Thou shalt have nothing but the forfeiture,
To be so taken at thy peril, Jew.

Shylock   Why, then the devil give him good of it!
I'll stay no longer question.

Portia Tarry, Jew:
The law hath yet another hold on you.
It is enacted in the laws of Venice,
If it be prov'd against an alien
That by direct or indirect attempts
He seek the life of any citizen,
The party 'gainst the which he doth contrive
Shall seize one half his goods; the other half
Comes to the privy coffer of the state;
And the offender's life lies in the mercy
Of the duke only, 'gainst all other voice.
In which predicament, I say, thou stand'st;
For it appears by manifest proceeding,
That indirectly and directly too
Thou hast contriv'd against the very life
Of the defendant; and thou hast incurr'd
The danger formerly by me rehears'd.
Down therefore and beg mercy of the duke.
(Act 4, Scene 1)

ACT TWO

Crimes and
Criminals

ACT TWO

Crimes and Criminals

PRODUCTION ACTIVITY

Once you have read this extract, predict the outcomes of the scene. Then consider some of the production elements needed to make it successful for an audience to watch. With your teacher's help, set up the classroom as a formal courtroom, and choose a cast to perform the scene. Divide into groups, each group focusing on a different aspect of the production. One group, for example, could consider costume, another the courtroom setting; smaller groups could each take one of the main characters and give the actors advice on how to present their characters. There might be other production factors for people to consider as well. Try to complete the scene in your own words, and then look at how it really ended.

How would the media have handled the event? Write a headline and opening sentence for your local newspaper; the opening lines of your local television station's report; or the opening questions in a radio interview with Antonio, Shylock, or Portia immediately after the court's decision had been announced.

THINK

After the performance, discuss what issues the production has brought out in relation to themes and character portrayal.

For example:

—Consider who gains the audience's sympathy.

—Has the court been fair?

—Have we seen "the letter of the law" in operation, or "the spirit of justice"?

—Has justice been done?

From Measure for Measure

This play revolves around the contrasts that exist sometimes between people's public and private lives. In this play, a wise duke is aware that his city needs some reforming, especially some tightening up on moral issues. For example, he thinks that prostitution in the city should be cleared up—and various other things as well. He fears that he may not be the right person to deal with the problems, so he goes on leave for some weeks leaving his deputy Angelo, who is a very "hard line" sort of person, in charge.

Angelo begins the task, part of which includes arresting two citizens, Claudio and Juliet, who have conceived a child "out of wedlock." Claudio's friends get together to help him and decide that the best person to approach Angelo to ask for his mercy would be Claudio's sister, Isabella, who is about to enter a convent. They think her innocence will make a good impression on Angelo. It does!—In fact, so much so that Angelo falls in love with her and tries to persuade her to have an affair with him. In return, he says, he will release Claudio.

Crimes and Criminals

Isabella is shocked and refuses, much to everyone's amazement. Great pressure is put on her to change her mind. Other murky details about Angelo's past emerge as well, and Claudio's life looks very much in peril. In some surprising twists, the original duke returns in disguise to discover what is going on. With Isabella's help—though not without risk to various people—he is finally able to expose Angelo and return to his rightful place.

You and your teacher might like to look at some extracts (particularly Act 1, Scene 2) from *Measure for Measure*. In fact, in many of Shakespeare's plays—especially the ones called tragedies—separating out those who are guilty and those who are innocent is extremely difficult and causes many hours of discussion and debate. There are crimes done for the good of someone or something, personal crimes, political crimes, and many others. You will find all this out as you experience more of Shakespeare's plays, either in stage performances, films, or class readings.

THINK

Many more moral dilemmas arise in this play:

—*Should Isabella sacrifice herself for her brother's life?*

—*Claudio is guilty under the laws of the city. Should he expect his sister to do this for him?*

—*The duke's abandonment of his people leaves them in the hands of a ruthless and corrupt man. Should he have left them? Why didn't he take the responsibility himself to clean up the city? Why did he want someone else to do his dirty work?*

—*When people are in public positions, should their own private lives be under public scrutiny?*

ACT THREE

Women of Words

Challenging Convention

This section gives you an opportunity to look broadly at some of the women of words Shakespeare presents to us. You will have a chance to speak their speeches and stage them; comment on the situations in which some of these women find themselves and explore what you might do in such circumstances; and, of course, gain an insight into why these parts are some of the most sought after in the world of theater.

There's no doubt Shakespeare wrote good parts for women—even though when he wrote them the women's parts were performed by boys! Even so, the parts for women, like the parts for men, tend to be strong, challenging, and complex.

Desdemona, Portia, Isabella, Lady Macbeth, Cordelia, Viola, Katherine, Beatrice, Cleopatra, Juliet, and Rosalind are some of the most famous Shakespearean women characters. How should we, as modern readers, view these Shakespearean women?

Women of Words

In Shakespeare's time, Renaissance women had few of the opportunities that are possible today to take leadership roles, to have careers, to do any sort of education or occupation that took them away from the domestic spheres of living. However, in his plays, Shakespeare has created many women characters who challenge the conventions of his time. (True, they usually have to be in disguise as men to do the unusual things—as we saw earlier on with the character of Portia in *The Merchant of Venice*.)

Because she uses a disguise as a young male lawyer, Portia is not criticized for her actions. Portia is unusual in other ways, in that she has control over her own financial and social life: her father has died leaving her a very wealthy young woman. She is not dependent on anyone. She has her own house. She never needs to seek permission for what she does. Olivia, in *Twelfth Night*, is another example of a woman able to exercise control over her own life because she has been left financially independent.

This is not true for all his women characters, however, many of whom are dependent on other people for their livelihood. Even so, some of these women do act differently from the normal expected patterns for women of their time.

ACT THREE

Women of Words

Nurse	Jesu, what haste! Can you not stay a while? Do you not see that I am out of breath?
Juliet	How art thou out of breath when thou hast breath To say to me that thou art out of breath? Th' excuse that thou dost make in this delay Is longer than the tale thou dost excuse. Is thy news good or bad? Answer to that. Say either, and I'll stay the circumstance. Let me be satisfied, is't good or bad?
Nurse	Well, you have made a simple choice, you know not how to choose a man. Romeo! No, not he. Though his face be better than any man's, yet his leg excels all men's—and for a hand and a foot and a body, though they be not to be talked on, yet they are past compare. He is not the flower of courtesy, but I'll warrant him as gentle as a lamb. Go thy ways, wench, serve God. What! have you din'd at home?
Juliet	No, no. But all this did I know before. What says he of our marriage, what of that?
Nurse	Lord, how my head aches! What a head have I! It beats as it would fall in twenty pieces. My back a t'other side—ah, my back, my back! Beshrew your heart for sending me about To catch my death with jauncing up and down.
Juliet	I' faith, I'm sorry that thou art not well. Sweet, sweet, sweet Nurse, tell me, what says my love?
Nurse	Your love says, like an honest gentleman, And a courteous, and a kind, and a handsome, And, I warrant, a virtuous—Where is your mother?

ACT THREE

Women of Words

Juliet	Where is my mother: why, she is within.
	Where should she be? How oddly thou repliest!
	"Your love says like an honest gentleman,
	'Where is your mother?'"
Nurse	O God's Lady dear!
	Are you so hot? Marry come up, I trow.
	Is this the poultice for my aching bones?
	Henceforward do your messages yourself.
Juliet	Here's such a coil! Come, what says Romeo?
Nurse	Have you got leave to go to shrift today?
Juliet	I have.
Nurse	Then hie you hence to Friar Laurence' cell,
	There stays a husband to make you a wife.
	Now comes the wanton blood up in your cheeks,
	They'll be in scarlet straight at any news.
	Hie you to church. I must another way,
	To fetch a ladder by the which your love
	Must climb a bird's nest soon when it is dark.
	I am the drudge and toil in your delight,
	But you shall bear the burden soon at night.
	Go, I'll to dinner. Hie you to the cell.
Juliet	Hie to high fortune! Honest Nurse, farewell.
	(Act 2, Scene 4)

> **jaunce**
> = journey
>
> **shrift**
> = to go to confession
>
> **marry come up, I trow**
> = by the Virgin Mary, wait a moment I trust
>
> **(these are expressions of irritation)**

THINK, WRITE, AND DESIGN

• *Try casting a boy as the Nurse. What difference does this make to the part?*

• *Make up the scene that might follow this. Imagine that the Nurse is having a chat with the cook of the Capulet household. During the chat, she talks about her meeting with Romeo, her thoughts about Juliet's secret marriage, and why she took her time telling Juliet the news. Make the scene humorous. Use your own language.*

• *Design the kind of costume that the Nurse might have worn on her errand to Romeo (she would have been wanting to look her best). Then look at Act 2, Scene 4, lines 82–88 in the play.*

ACT THREE

Women of Words

From Antony and Cleopatra

CLEOPATRA

The story of Antony and Cleopatra is one of the most famous love stories of all time—and it's also true. Set against the backdrop of ancient Egypt, it is a grand story of exotic passion! You might even have seen it famously brought to the screen by Richard Burton and Elizabeth Taylor. It's definitely worth having a look at part of this old movie to get a feel for the scale of this story. Why is it so grand and full of passion? Mainly because of the location (Egypt) and the reputation of its fiery heroine (Cleopatra).

THINK AND WRITE

What do you already know about ancient Egypt? Brainstorm everything you know on the board with your class. At this stage, it will probably just be odd words and images. Next, brainstorm any questions you have about this period of history. Then add any details you know about the historical figure Cleopatra. Can anyone else in the class answer the questions which have come up? Spend some time in the library seeing if you can extend your knowledge of this period and finding out about Cleopatra.

When Shakespeare decided to turn this story into a play, it was already a well-known tale. He would have known of the story from a famous Greek book called *Parallel Lives* by Plutarch (A.D. c.46–126), a writer and philosopher. Rather like many screenwriters today, Shakespeare got most of his stories from already "available sources" rather than making up the stories himself. You have probably seen many films that have been adapted from novels. Well, Shakespeare adapted written works in this way for his plays. Not all of his plays, of course, but you will find, if you research the lives of some of the famous people about whom he wrote, that much in the stories are factually correct. He took the factual story, then invented other characters who add to the plot and themes, created motives, and compacted the life and times of whomever into a two- or three-hour stage play. This is what he does with Mark Antony and Queen Cleopatra, who really did have a love affair that, centuries ago, led to their demises.

HOW DID THEY MEET?

This is not a typical boy-meets-girl story. In fact, by the time Antony and Cleopatra got together, Antony had been married five times (though Shakespeare conveniently ignores this!). The love story is set in the time of the Roman Empire. At this time, a large portion of the known world was administered by the Romans and divided into a number of parts. Each part was administered by a Roman general. Mark Antony had the Eastern Mediterranean as his responsibility, and this is how he came to meet the most famous queen of Egypt, Cleopatra.

Much has been made of how involved the soldier, Mark Antony, was with this exotic queen. Even the history books show that he cared less and less about his role as a governor and more about his relationship with the queen as time went on. Shakespeare takes this theme of giving up everything for love as the basis for the play he writes about them. He also focuses on the legendary beauty of Cleopatra and her fiery nature. It is Cleopatra's combination of beauty and fire that Shakespeare highlights as being both frightening and irresistible.

Women of Words

A FEARFUL BEAUTY

Shakespeare presents Cleopatra as a woman of many moods. She can be charming, cunning, funny, noble, and angry within the space of a few scenes. But one constant that she does have is the ability to make people sit up and take notice. Look at the way she is described as she sits in the royal barge on a trip down the River Nile. Cleopatra clearly liked to make an impression!

> The barge she sat in, like a burnish'd throne
> Burn't on the water: the poop was beaten gold,
> Purple the sails, and so perfumed that
> The winds were lovesick with them; the oars were silver,
> Which to the tune of flutes kept stroke, and made
> The water which they beat to follow faster,
> As amorous of their strokes. For her own person,
> It beggar'd all description; she did lie
> In her pavilion, cloth of gold of tissue—
> O'er-picturing that Venus where we see
> The fancy outwork nature. On each side her

ACT THREE

Women of Words

Stood pretty dimpled boys, like smiling Cupids,
With divers-color'd fans, whose wind did seem
To glow the delicate cheeks which they did cool,
And what they undid did.

(Act 2, Scene 2)

READ THROUGH

Now read this next short extract that shows another side to Cleopatra's character. Here, a messenger comes with the news that, while on a trip back to Rome, Antony has married, for political reasons, Octavia, the sister of Caesar. Because the messenger is afraid of how she might react, he takes his time to break the news. By the time he tells her, Cleopatra has worked herself into a frenzy of frustration.

Messenger Madam, he's married to Octavia.

Cleopatra The most infectious pestilence upon thee!
[Strikes him down]

Messenger Good madam, patience.

Cleopatra What say you?
[Strikes him again]

        Hence, horrible villain, or I'll spurn thine eyes
        Like balls before me; I'll unhair thy head:
[She hales him up and down]
        Thou shalt be whipp'd with wire, and stew'd in brine,
        Smarting in ling'ring pickle.

Messenger Gracious madam,
        I that do bring the news made not the match.

ACT THREE

Women of Words

Cleopatra   Say 'tis not so, a province I will give thee,
And make thy fortunes proud: the blow thou hadst
Shall make thy peace for moving me to rage,
And I will boot thee with what gift beside
Thy modesty can beg.

Messenger He's married, madam.

Cleopatra   Rogue, thou hast liv'd too long.
[Draws a knife]

Messenger Nay, then I'll run.
[Exit]
(Act 2, Scene 5)

Later, Cleopatra sends the same messenger to see what Octavia is like. He comes back some time later with this report. Note how he has learned his lesson! (Charmian is Cleopatra's handmaid.)

Cleopatra   Didst thou behold Octavia?

Messenger Ay, dread queen.

Cleopatra   Where?

Messenger Madam, in Rome;
I look'd her in the face, and saw her led
Between her brother and Mark Antony.

Cleopatra   Is she as tall as me?

Messenger She is not, madam.

Cleopatra   Didst hear her speak? Is she shrill-tongu'd or low?

Messenger Madam, I heard her speak; she is low-voiced.

ACT THREE

Women of Words

Cleopatra That's not so good. He cannot like her long.

Charmian Like her! O Isis! 'tis impossible.

Cleopatra I think so, Charmian: dull of tongue, and dwarfish!
What majesty is in her gait? Remember,
If e'er thou look'st on majesty.

Messenger She creeps:
Her motion and her station are as one;
She shows a body rather than a life,
A statue than a breather.

Cleopatra Is this certain?

Messenger Or I have no observance.

Charmian Three in Egypt
Cannot make better note.

Cleopatra He's very knowing,
I do perceive't. There's nothing in her yet.
The fellow has good judgment.

Charmian Excellent.

Cleopatra Guess at her years, I prithee.

Messenger Madam, she was a widow.

Cleopatra Widow! Charmian, hark.

Messenger And I do think she's thirty.

Cleopatra Bear'st thou her face in mind? is't long or round?

Messenger Round even to faultiness.

Cleopatra For the most part, too, they are foolish that
are so.
Her hair, what color?

Messenger Brown, madam: and her forehead
As low as she would wish it.

Cleopatra There's gold for thee:
Thou must not take my former sharpness ill.
I will employ thee back again; I find thee
Most fit for business.
(Act 3, Scene 3)

ACT THREE

Women of Words

In stage productions, at the point when the messenger says, "And I do think she's thirty," Cleopatra often briefly pauses before delivering her next line, and the audience usually laughs. Why do you think this is?

As a class, discuss what kind of woman you think Cleopatra is. Bear in mind that you have only had a taste of what she is really like. Although you might have been amused by this selection, remember that in the play she is a noble and tragic character. Ultimately, when Antony dies and she is without his protection, she is captured by Caesar. She kills herself rather than live as a prisoner and without Antony.

WRITE AND DESIGN

Look back through these extracts and select altogether about twenty words or phrases that appeal to you. You might like the sound of them or the images they create. Write them clearly, using interesting colors and script, on a piece of card and cut them out. Rearrange them randomly on a piece of contruction paper so that you create a visual impression of Cleopatra's character. Illustrate your work.

ACT THREE

Women of Words

From Much Ado About Nothing
BEATRICE

Beatrice in *Much Ado About Nothing* is a clever woman who slightly terrifies everyone with her sharpness. She has been brought up in her uncle's house and provides a striking contrast to her much more traditional and milder cousin, Hero. She is unusual for Shakespeare's times for the equality she demands for herself, and especially for her wit and intellect.

Her uncle, Leonato, tries to encourage her to get married, not because he wants rid of her, but because he believes it is the best for young women of her age. For example, in Act 2, Scene 1, he says:

Leonato   By my troth, niece, thou wilt never get thee a husband, if thou be so shrewd of thy tongue.

When her uncle says that he hopes she will one day be "fitted with a husband," she makes a typical sharp reply:

Beatrice   Not till God make men of some other metal than earth. Would it not grieve a woman to be over-mastered with a piece of valiant dust to make an account of her life to a clod of wayward marl? No, uncle, I'll none: Adam's sons are my brethren; and truly, I hold it a sin to match in my kindred.

In addition to this example, Beatrice is frequently discussed by others for her sharpness. They see her as very unusual and describe her, for example, as "My dear Lady Disdain," or "In faith, she's too curst," or "she speaks poinards and every word is stabs." Her wit and cleverness are a constant source for discussion among her friends and family.

BEATRICE FOR BENEDICK

Beatrice has for some time been feuding in fun with Benedick, a popular young lord from Padua. They constantly tease and abuse each other in sharp-witted language that sometimes cuts very close to the bone. Some of the most entertaining scenes in the play are the verbal jousting which goes on between them. Here are some examples:

Benedick has just returned from the wars and is greeting his friends when Beatrice notices him.

Women of Words

Beatrice   I wonder that you will still be talking, Signior Benedick: nobody marks you.

Benedick   What! my dear Lady Disdain, are you yet living?

Beatrice   Is it possible Disdain should die while she hath such meet food to feed it as Signior Benedick? Courtesy itself must convert to disdain, if you come in her presence.

Benedick   Then is courtesy a turncoat. But it is certain I am loved of all ladies, only you excepted; and I would I could find in my heart that I had not a hard heart; for truly, I love none.

Beatrice   A dear happiness to women: they would else have been troubled with a pernicious suitor. I thank God and my cold blood. I am of your humour for that: I had rather hear my dog bark at a crow than a man swear he loves me.

Benedick   God keep your ladyship still in that mind! So some gentleman or other shall 'scape a predestinate scratched face.

---

mark
= to take notice of

Courtesy ... presence
= even courtesy herself would be rude to you

dear happiness
= great good luck

scape ... face
= escape getting his face scratched

parrot-teacher
= great chatterer

so ... continuer
= able to keep going on

jade
= a worn-out horse, or old run-down nag

ACT THREE

Women of Words

Beatrice Scratching could not make it worse, and 'twere such a face as yours were.

Benedick Well, you are a rare parrot-teacher.

Beatrice A bird of my tongue is better than a beast of yours.

Benedick I would my horse had the speed of your tongue.

(Act I, Scene 1)

Another example of their banter occurs at a masked ball organized to celebrate the safe return of the Duke's soldiers from war. In this instance, although they are supposed to be in disguise and unrecognizable to each other because of the masks they are wearing, both Beatrice and Benedick have recognized each other but are pretending that they haven't.

Beatrice Will you not tell me who told you so?

Benedick No, you shall pardon me.

Beatrice Nor will you not tell me who you are?

Benedick Not now.

Beatrice That I was disdainful, and that I had my good wit out of the "Hundred Merry Tales." Well, this was Signior Benedick that said so.

Benedick What's he?

Beatrice I am sure you know him well enough.

Benedick Not I, believe me.

Beatrice Did he never make you laugh?

Benedick   I pray you, what is he?

Beatrice   Why, he is the prince's jester: a very dull fool; only his gift is in devising impossible slanders: none but libertines delight in him; and the commendation is not in his wit, but in his villainy; for he both pleases men and angers them, and then they laugh at him and beat him. I am sure he is in the fleet: I would he had boarded me!

Benedick   When I know the gentleman, I'll tell him what you say.

Beatrice   Do, do: he'll but break a comparison or two on me; which, peradventure not marked or not laughed at, strikes him into melancholy; and then there's a partridge wing saved, for the fool will eat no supper that night.

[Music for the dance]
We must follow the leaders.

Benedick   In every good thing.

Beatrice   Nay, if they lead to any ill, I will leave them at the next turning.
(Act 2, Scene 1)

ACT THREE

Women of Words

The Hundred Merry Tales
= was a well-known book of jokes

libertines
= good for nothings

fleet
= company or crowd of people

but break a comparison
= just make a few smart remarks

partridge wing
= just a tiny piece

ACT THREE

Women of
Words

PRODUCTION ACTIVITY

Prepare for a performance of one of these scenes for the rest of the class. Divide into small groups and first, as a group, go through the language carefully to make sure you have understood the extent of the jokes and trade of insults. You might need to use the notes provided to help with some of the Shakespearean slang and colloquial language. Your teacher will help to interpret the text. You might like to think of what some of these expressions would be in today's slang.

Choose two actors to play the roles, and the rest of the group should help to work out how it would be best performed. Remember you want to play the scene for as many laughs and clever insults as you can. These two characters, especially Beatrice, really enjoy the slinging of insults at each other.

Perform the scenes for the class. Discuss the performances, comparing the different interpretations given by different actors and the ways in which the humor has been brought out.

In these examples of the battle of jokes and traded insults between Beatrice and Benedick, which of the two characters scores the most points over the other? Who do you think is the wittier and more clever?

Another of Shakespeare's comic plays also has a woman character famous for her blunt speaking and independent behavior, especially in relation to men. Do you know which one it is? It is a play which has contributed a lot of negative language and jokes about strong women.

In the relations between the sexes today, how acceptable is it for a woman to be sharpwitted in the company of men? Do we accept women who are more clever than men? Think about these issues in relation to famous people such as men political leaders and their partners, as well as in your relations with members of the opposite sex.

By the way, *Much Ado About Nothing* is one of Shakespeare's most famous comedies, so, as well as having lots of comic scenes in it, it also has a happy ending. Part of its happy ending is that Beatrice and Benedick, with a little help from their friends, eventually fall in love and get married. Would you have expected this from what you have seen of the two characters so far? You might ask your teacher to show you some scenes from the Kenneth Branagh film of the play if you want to know more about how this comes to pass.

The Epilogue

Getting to Know Shakespeare has been written to give you a taste of Shakespeare's talents, an introduction to his many stories and characters, and a look at his skills as an entertainer and teller of mysterious tales. Through his words, he continues to live in our culture even though he died four hundred years ago. Often people ask why we should still read Shakespeare and how his work could still be relevant in today's world. Do you have any answers to these questions?

Perhaps you could end this unit of work with a class debate or discussion on the value to be gained from a study of Shakespeare's life and works. Use this as the basis for an essay on the same topic.

For further innovative approaches to teaching Shakespeare, you may want to refer to the following resources:

- Rathgen, Elody and Pauline Scanlan. *Say It With Words.* Caxton Educational, 1991.

- Robbins, Mari Lu. *Interdisciplinary Unit: Shakespeare.* Teacher Created Resources, 1995.

In addition, enter the following **key words** into an Internet search engine for more information on the life and work of William Shakespeare:

- Shakespeare

- Stratford-on-Avon

- Globe theater

- Bard

- Hamlet

- sonnets

One indication of Shakespeare's influence on popular culture is the number of films that have been adapted from his plays. The following list offers a few examples of the over 250 cinematic adaptations of the Bard's work.

Hamlet

- (1948) starring Lawrence Olivier

- (1964) starring Richard Burton

- (1991) starring Mel Gibson

- (1996) starring Kenneth Branagh

Othello

- (1952) directed by and starring Orson Welles

- (1965) starring Lawrence Olivier

- (1995) starring Laurence Fishburne

Romeo and Juliet

- (1935) directed by George Cukor

- (1968) directed by Franco Zeffirelli

- (1996) directed by Baz Luhrman

Other films inspired by Shakespeare:

- *Ran* (1985) directed by Akira Kurosawa

- *Rosencrantz and Guildenstern Are Dead* (1991) written and directed by Tom Stoppard

- *Looking for Richard* (1996) directed by Al Pacino

- *Shakespeare in Love* (1998) starring Gwyneth Paltrow